CW00539384

ROMMEL'S DESERT WARRIORS 1941-42

ROMMEL'S DESERT WARRIORS 1941-42

MICHAEL OLIVE & ROBERT EDWARDS

Pen & Sword
MILITARY

First published in the United States of America in 2012 by Stackpole Books

First printed in Great Britain in 2012 by
PEN & SWORD MILITARY
an imprint of
Pen & Sword Books Ltd,
47 Church Street,
Barnsley,
South Yorkshire.
S70 2AS

A CIP record for this book is available from the British Library.

ISBN 978 1 84884 866 5

Printed in the United States of America

Pen & Sword Books Ltd incorporates the Imprints of Pen & Sword Aviation,
Pen & Sword Family History, Pen & Sword Maritime, Pen & Sword Military,
Pen & Sword Discovery, Pen & Sword Politics, Pen & Sword Atlas,
Pen & Sword Archaeology, Wharncliffe Local History, Wharncliffe True Crime,
Wharncliffe Transport, Pen & Sword Select, Pen & Sword Military Classics,
Leo Cooper, The Praetorian Press, Claymore Press, Remember When,
Seaforth Publishing and Frontline Publishing

For a complete list of Pen & Sword titles please contact
Pen & Sword Books Limited
47 Church Street, Barnsley, South Yorkshire, S70 2AS, England
E-mail: enquiries@pen-and-sword.co.uk
Website: www.pen-and-sword.co.uk

CONTENTS

Foreword vii

Introduction viii

ARRIVAL IN THE DESERT 2

COMMUNICATIONS 13

ARMORED VEHICLES 33

SUPPLY BATTALION 68

THE LUFTWAFFE AND REGIA AERONAUTICA 82

ROMMEL 98

ARTILLERY 105

LIFE IN THE DESERT 113

TRANSPORT VEHICLES 171

Appendices 189

Select Bibliography 195

Acknowledgments 197

FOREWORD

"There exists a real danger that our friend Rommel is becoming a kind of magical or bogey-man to our troops." Indeed, German General Erwin Rommel earned his Desert Fox nickname by employing bold, risky tactics that saw him best much larger enemy formations while avoiding what often appeared to be certain defeat time and again. Rommel, however, was far from perfect. While his unpredictability proved a tricky thorn to the British, Rommel's own forces often didn't know where the wily Desert Fox was or what he was up to. This produced worrying confusion among his own headquarters staff, distrust among his Italian allies, and complaints from his superiors, who thought he was in over his head. Still, Claude Auchinleck, the British general in command of the 8th Army in North Africa—and for a time Rommel's counterpart in the see-saw battle that raged across the desert—was having a difficult time convincing his troops that Rommel and his vaunted Afrika Korps were merely men and, more importantly, men who could be beaten.

The Deutsches Afrika Korps (DAK) began humbly enough, arriving piecemeal in Africa beginning in February 1941 to act as a small supporting force for the beleaguered Italian Army that was on the verge of being run out of Africa by the British. No one, least of all Adolf Hitler, expected the newly formed DAK to do much more than stabilize the situation. In fact, Rommel's orders were not to attack, but to wait until more forces arrived. Rommel didn't listen, and an Italian rout became a British one, with the Desert Fox nipping at their heels.

In *Rommel's Desert Warriors*, the stark beauty of the North African desert is revealed in original photographs taken by the German soldiers who fought there. It's worth remembering as you look through the book that the war in the desert was fought across the vast Sahara (an Arabic word which simply means "desert") in temperatures that ranged in excess of 110 degrees Fahrenheit to below freezing conditions at night. Sandstorms, known locally as *simoom*—"poison wind"—scoured the desert floor, creating blinding clouds of skin-abrading sand. Water was scarce and navigation exceptionally difficult in a landscape that changed rapidly. It was a hellish place to fight a war, yet the North African campaign became one known for its chivalry.

New photographs of Rommel himself give additional insight into the warrior who so perplexed his allies and enemies. From panzers churning across the sand to fortified positions made of rock, the photographs capture what it was like to live and fight in one of the harshest climates on the planet. In order to survive, let alone prevail, the German Army issued specialized uniforms and weapons for the desert environment. Once again, we include an eight-page color spread depicting original items from the North African campaign. And throughout the book, German military history experts Robert Edwards and Michael Olive add context and detail to the hundreds of photos presented here.

Rommel and the Afrika Korps hold a hallowed place in military history. They fought in an unforgiving environment against overwhelming odds, and though their ultimate fate would be defeat, they nonetheless wrote their names into the history books as one of the most daring fighting forces to ever go to war. Here, in *Rommel's Desert Warriors*, you'll see why.

Chris Evans
Editor
Stackpole Books

INTRODUCTION

On 8 February 1942, British units of the Western Desert Force, under the command of General Sir Richard O'Connor, were on the frontier between Cyrenaica and Tripolitania. The strategic port of Tripoli was under threat, and there was the possibilty that the Italians could be ejected from North Africa.

The attempted Italian invasion of Egypt by Marshal Rodolpho Graziani's 10th Army had ended in disaster. Forty thousand Commonwealth troops had taken over 130,00 Italian prisioners and occupied Cyrenaica.

In order to assist their Axis partner, the Germans decided to step in. The mission was to to be strictly defensive in nature.

According to War Directive No. 22, German support for battles in the Mediterranean area was required:

The situation in the Mediterranean area, where England is employing superior forces against our allies, requires that Germany should assist for reasons of strategy, politics, and psychology. Tripolitania must be held and the danger of a collapse on the Albanian front must be eliminated.

I therefore order as follows:

Commander in Chief Army will provide covering forces sufficient to render valuable service to our allies in the defense of Tripolitania, particualrly against British armored divisions. Special orders for the composition of this force will follow.[1]

The North African operation was given the code name *Sonnenblume* (Sunflower). Relatively modest German forces were proposed, consisting of two *Panzer* divisions: the *5. leichte Division* consisting of cadres from the *3. Panzer-Division* plus its *Panzer-Regiment 5;* and the *15. Panzer-Division.*

Command of these formations was entrusted to *Generalleutant* Erwin Rommel. Rommel had won fame in France as commander of the *7. Panzer-Division.* His division had moved so rapidly and maneuvered so skillfully that it was nicknamed the "Ghost Division." The German forces in Africa were to receive the title *Deutsches Afrikakorps (DAK)*, and a legend was born.

From the time that Rommel arrived in Tripoli, on 12 February 1941, the war in Africa changed dramatically. Without waiting for the bulk of his forces to arrive, Rommel decided to go on the offensive.

The 1941–42 North African campaign was fought along a fairly narrow coastal strip of some 1,200 miles (1,900 kilometers) from El Agheila to El Alamein. Both the Axis and Allied forces

---

1. Hugh Trevor-Roper, ed., *Hitler's War Directives, 1939–1945* (London, 1966), 98–101.

involved were, at least at the begining of the campaign, relatively small in number.

The fighting was hard but generally conducted in a fair manner. Prisioners were well treated, and enemy wounded received appropriate medical treatment. There was a mutual respect between the German and Commonwealth forces that extended from the common soldier to general officers. Both sides shared the hardships and privations of the desert environment. There was little of the animosity that characterized the later campaigns in Italy and Europe.

The British, in particular, have tended to romanticize the desert war. North Africa was a relatively "clean" conflict, with few civilian casualties and very little destruction of civilian property. The soldiers of the *Afrikakorps* and the "Desert Rats" of the 8th Army have achieved legendary status.

On 24 March 1941, while his forces were still in the process of assembling, Rommel attacked toward El Agheila with parts of the *5. leichte Division* and two Italian divisions. The British forces were disorganized, dispersed, and short of supplies. In addition, General Wavell had to withdraw a large number of troops for the ill-fated expedition to Greece. General Neame was left with only a covering force.

By 2 April, Rommel was in Agedabia, with the Italians moving toward Derna. On 10 April, Rommel launched an assault on the fortress of Tobruk, held by the Australian 7th Division. This attack and a larger assault on 14 April were thrown back. A cordon of Italian toops was thrown around Tobruk, and Rommel continued his advance. On 30 April, a full-scale attack was launched to capture Tobruk but, other than creating a small salient, was unsuccessful.

With a mixture of surprise, daring maneuvers, bluff, and tactical brilliance, Rommel countered the British "Brevity" (May) and "Battleaxe" (June) offensives.

Operation "Crusader" opened on 18 November with the intention of finally destroying the *Afrikakorps*. "Crusader" was a long, confusing battle with numerous attacks and counterattacks. When it started, Rommel was occupied with Tobruk, and *Generalleutnant* Crüwell was in command of the *Afrikakorps*. Rommel soon reestablished command. On 24 November, Rommel made a "dash to the wire" to relieve the embattled Halfaya garrison and cut off the 8th Army.

This attack was unsuccessful. Rommel initiated a tactical withdrawal, and the *DAK* arrived at Mersa el Brega on 2 January 1942. Able to build up his troops, equipment, and supplies more quickly than the British, Rommel attacked on 21 January 1942 with only 117 German and 79 Italian tanks. On 5–6 February, the British Gazala Line was reached, and both sides consolidated and built up their strength for four months.

Characteristically, Rommel took the initiative, attacking to the south, while Crüwell feinted an attack in the north. Despite initial success, things did not go well for Rommel, and the *DAK* was in danger of being destroyed. However, the commander of the 8th Army, General Sir Neil Ritchie, failed to take advantage of the situation, and Rommel won a brilliant victory at Gazala. The 8th Army retreated in disorder to the Marsa Matruh Line.

There was to be no repeat of his failure to take Tobruk in 1941. Three Axis armored divisions launched a coordinated assault on 20 June, and by 21 June, Tobruk had fallen, with 30,000 Commonwealth troops taken prisoner. This was to be the high point of Rommel's military career.

General Sir Claude Auchinleck sacked Ritchie and took over direct command of the 8th Army. A delaying action was fought at the Marsa Matruh Line, and Auchinleck retreated to a defensive position at the insignificant railway station at El Alamein.

Rommel pushed his tired and depleted formations to defeat the 8th Army and advance on Alexandria, only some sixty miles away. In the first battle of El Alamein, Auchinleck proved to be the equal of Rommel by adopting a flexible defense and not allowing him to gain the initiative. The battle ended in a stalemate, and both sides dug in. The British forces were being rapidly resupplied and heavily reinforced, being so close to their principal base of operations.

Rommel could not wait for the inevitable resumption of British offensive operations. There was one more attempt at attacking the 8th Army at the battle of Alam Halfa, launched on the night of 30–31 August. However, the new commander of the 8th Army, General Sir Bernard Montgomery, held firm. A lack of fuel for his *Panzers* finally compelled Rommel to withdraw to his original position.

Aircraft and naval units from Malta were playing havoc with Rommel's supplies, and only a fraction of what was necessary to just maintain an adequate defense was getting through. With characteristic energy, Rommel strengthened the El Alamein position, planting thousands of mines in his "Devil's Garden." Montgomery would not be rushed into a premature offensive and methodically built up his forces until they attained overwhelming strength.

The 8th Army finally reached a strength of 195,000 combat troops and over 1,000 tanks, including 400 of the new M4 Sherman, and 2,000 guns. The Axis forces had 50,000 German and 60,000 Italian troops and about 500 tanks, of which 275 were Italian and, therefore, almost useless.

On 23 October, the second battle of El Alamein began with a massive barrage by over 1,000 guns. Rommel was in Germany when the battle began and did not return until the second day. The German and Italian soldiers fought gallantly, but ultimately, there was no stopping the relentless onslaught. Disobeying Hitler's order to stand fast, Rommel ordered a retreat on the night of 3–4 November, leaving the largely non-motorized Italian troops, who had defended their positions with conspicuous courage, to their fate. The long road back, which would eventually lead to Tunisia, had begun.

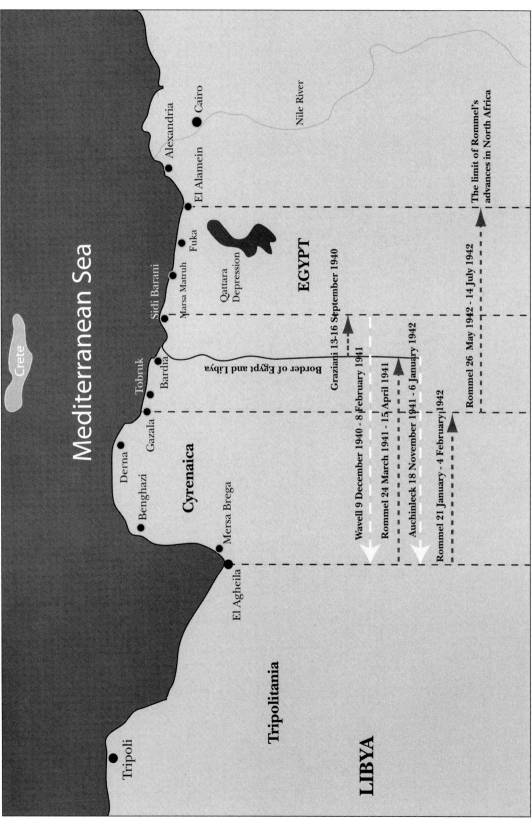

This overall map of the North African campaign illustrates the back-and-forth nature of the conflict. Offensive operations were followed by counteroffensives.

ARRIVAL IN THE DESERT

Fleets of *Junkers Ju 52* transport aircraft ferrying essential German military personnel from the Italian mainland or Sicily to Tripoli. Slow and vulnerable, the *Ju 52's* were heavily escorted by fighters. It is evident that these flights were undertaken at extremely low altitude.

The cramped conditions inside the *Ju 52*. The strictly utilitarian "Aunty Ju" lacked any concession to creature comforts.

This page and the next: Safe arrival in a new theater of war: North Africa, a far cry from the green fields and mild climate of Western Europe

Heavy equipment and enlisted men traveled by ship from Italy or Sicily. In the early days of the campaign, with Malta under heavy attack by the *Luftwaffe*, most convoys got through relatively unscathed. The convoys were heavily escorted by Italian naval units with a ratio of two escort vessels to every cargo vessel. This was a ratio that the Allies never achieved. In the later stages of the campaign, strike aircraft and submarines from Malta caused havoc with these convoys, starving the *Afrikakorps* of vital fuel and ammunition

Unloading of the communications unit's vehicles onto ferries. The seeming lack of extensive unloading facilities indicates that this is not a major port like Tripoli; it may be Bardia.

The new arrivals acclimatize to their somewhat exotic environment, meet the local populace, and, like the typical tourist, take photographs.

The imposing pedestals are distinctly Italian in character, indicating that this is a major city in Italian-colonized North Africa.

Setting up camp and preparing defenses. The war in the desert was often so fluid that an all-round defensive position was essential.

A break from arduous duty. One of the most important events of a soldier's day is mealtime.

An encounter with the local wildlife. Not all desert creatures were so harmless, however.

A *Panzer III Ausf. E* mounting the 3.7-cm *KwK L/46.5*.

COMMUNICATIONS

Medium cross-country communications trucks with their telescoping antennae. These vehicles were extensively used for intercepting enemy radio transmissions, providing German commanders with valuable intelligence. British radio discipline was notoriously lax.

As is obvious from the Italian-language signage, this is a town in Libya.

Two medium cross-country trucks and a medium cross-country personnel vehicle that is equipped with oversized desert tires to enhance traction and reduce heat build-up.

Mechanical problems in the desert could be fatal.

Establishing telegraph communications,
a seemingly never-ending task.

This page and the top of the next page:
A senior commanders conference with
none other than Rommel himself.
Rommel's plans were based on the
constantly changing circumstances of
battle.

A radio-intercept truck dug in and probably functioning as a listening post.

Another view of the truck on the previous page, with a closer look at the antenna array.

Striking a suitably impressive pose for the photo album. Although the desert conditions were harsh, it did not appear that the German soldiers were affected psychologically to the same extent as their comrades in Russia were by that vast, unforgiving landscape.

What appear to be self-propelled guns on flatbed trailers being towed by half-tracks.

A supply convoy on its long journey from the principal supply bases to the front. Logistics posed a huge problem for both British and German forces. As either side advanced, they soon encountered shortages of all the items required for a modern army as they outran their supply lines.

The remains of a destroyed supply convoy. As there was only one major highway in North Africa, the Via Balbia, it was comparatively easy to interdict enemy supply columns from the air.

The reason for the smoke in the background is unknown, but ominous. Note that the tent in the foreground is protected by a low stone wall. Death in the desert could come at any time.

Another view of the encampment shown above. A radio-intercept truck is in the background.

A dramatic photograph of the featureless desert plain. If there were no obvious tracks to follow, accurate navigation by sun compass or the stars was essential.

This soldier looks well pleased with his efforts to provide himself with protected living quarters.

A Fiat G50 bis fighter landing at a forward airfield. The G50 was inferior to the British Hawker Hurricane in the early days of the campaign.

A *Mittlerer Zugkraftwagen Sd.Kfz. 6/1,* used as a personel carrier, tow vehicle, engineer vehicle, and self-propelled platform for the *3.7-cm Flak 36.*

Erecting a substantial tent. Extensive camouflage is essential to protect the occupants from marauding Allied aircraft.

A fairly elaborate German and Italian military cemetery.

The unit's vehicles
near the coast.

A supply convoy's staging area at an oasis.

An award ceremony for the Iron Cross, Second Class.

Two more views of the unit's vehicles and personnel.
Left: Perhaps the soldier climbing the palm tree is stringing a telegraph line or just larking about.
Below: Two *Kfz. 17* radio cars.

Two *8.8-cm Flak 18* on their trailers. The stone wall may have been constructed to protect the guns in the antitank role.

Another view of the 88's along with a 1920s-vintage Rolls-Royce armored car of the British 10th Hussars.

A field latrine in its most primitive form.   Field-expedient cooking.

A captured British AEC "Mammoth" armored command vehicle sporting prominent German markings and nicknamed "Max." Rommel used this vehicle as his command post. The *Afrikakorps* made extensive use of captured Allied vehicles, pariculary motor transport.

A formidable looking group of *Afrikakorps* soldiers standing in front of their heavy truck and *Sd.Kfz. 6* half-track. The *esprit de corps* of both the *Afrikakorps* and the 8th Army was excellent.

A *Kübelwagen* in front of a field hospital. Generally, clearly marked hospitals and ambulance vehicles were respected by both sides.

An encampment in a relatively secluded oasis setting. Areas such as these were few and far between.

German and Italian troops gathering at a fairly substantial fortification, possibly at the Tobruk perimeter. They appear to be observing enemy positions.

A fine portrait of one of Rommel's desert warriors. Motorcycles were used extensively in the desert for reconnaissance and communications.

ARMORED VEHICLES

Trackless terrain such as this, with shifting sand and numerous dunes, was practically impossible to negotiate, even for tracked vehicles.

Panzers advancing at speed. The lead vehicle looks to be a *Panzer III.*

What appears to be a *2.0-cm Flak* in use against ground targets.

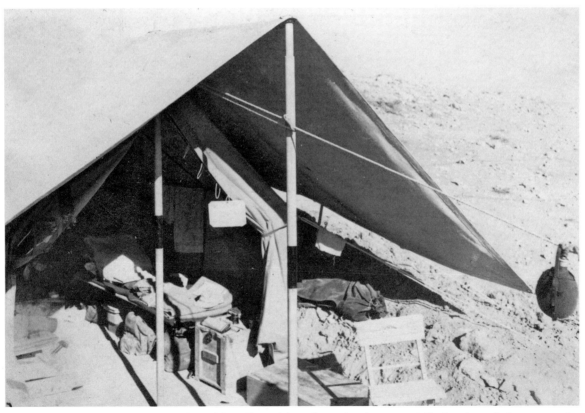

Accommodation desert style. Note how this well-provisioned tent has been partially dug in to help protect the occupants from bomb and artillery shrapnel.

Action on the horizon. With almost no concealment possible, enemy forces could be seen from long distances.

A close call. This is an impact from a light-caliber shell, perhaps a 2-pounder antitank round.

Three destroyed and burned-out Italian M13/40 tanks. Despite carrying a handy 4.7-cm main gun, this tank was poorly armored and mechanically unreliable.

A *Panzer IV*, probably an *Ausf. E* variant mounting the low-velocity 7.5-cm L/24 main gun. Intended primarily as an infantry-support vehicle, the L/24 gun was capable of penetrating the front armor of most British tanks at medium to short range.

The standard Italian medium tank the *M13/40/M13/41*. Thinly armored, underpowered, and unreliable, its one good feature was the reasonably effective 4.7-cm main gun.

An Italian *Carro Commando M41*, a command vehicle based on the M13/40 tank. Armament was a 13.2-mm heavy machine gun and an 8-mm machine gun.

Above and previous page: A *Panzer IV* and *Panzer III*, respectively, being unloaded in Tripoli. Both vehicles are still in their *Panzer* grey finish.

A newly arrived *Panzer IV, Ausführung D*, moves at speed across the desert. Movement-control numbers can still be seen marked in chalk on the front of the hull, and covers are still on the main gun and hull machine gun. One of the tankers is still wearing a black *Panzer* overseas cap, which was intended for wear in continental Europe.

A fake *Panzer II*, usually mounted on a Kubelwagen chassis, used to deceive British aerial reconnaissance. Deception efforts were widespread and imaginative on both sides during the fighting in North Africa.

The real thing: A *Panzer III* undergoing track maintenance. This *Ausf. G* model mounts the 5-cm L/42 main gun. Note the external stowage of canteens. The roadwheels are probably carried as spares rather than to supplement the frontal armor, which was more than adequate in the early days of the campaign.

A *Panzer III Ausf. G* mounting the shorter L/42 5-cm main gun. This weapon was capable of defeating most British tanks in the desert at that time. The frontal armor is supplemented with spare track links. Additional road wheels are carried; the rocky terrain was very hard on the rubber tires.

Two views of the standard Italian main battle tank, the M13/40 or M14/41 (only the power of the motor differed between models). The tank above appears to have developed engine trouble.

An *Afrikakorps* soldier strikes a relaxed pose. The M13/M14 had 37mm turret and 30mm hull armor. The 47mm main gun was a reasonably handy weapon but incapable of dealing with the heavier-model British tanks.

A later-model Italian tank, the M15/42, featured heavier armor, a more powerful engine, and a longer version of the 47mm main gun.

A late-model *Panzer III Ausf. L* with the long 5cm L/60 main gun. As Allied tank and antitank guns increased in caliber, additional armor protection in the form of track sections and sandbags was applied in the field.

A German and Italian soldier relax on what appears to be a wrecked AB 40 Italian armored car, although with the vehicle in this state it is hard to identify it with any certainty.

A disabled up-armored *Panzer II Ausf. C* that appears to have either hit a mine or suffered from an artillery strike. Both the German and British tank-recovery teams were very efficient. Possession of the battlefield therefore became very important as the victor's vehicles could be recovered and repaired and those of the enemy either captured and used against their former owners or destroyed to prevent recovery.

A dramatic and famous shot of an *Sd.Kfz. 250/3* command vehicle. The tactical symbol is for a towed artillery unit of 3rd Battery divisional artillery of the *5. leichte Division*. As a color image, it was featured on the covers of several propaganda magazines of the day.

The full crew of an *Sd.Kfz. 7*, complete with mascot. Dress regulations in the desert were somewhat relaxed.

An *Sd.Kfz. 7* half-track towing a 15-cm *sFH 18* howitzer. The *sFH 18* was the standard German heavy artillery piece.

An *Sd.Kfz. 251 Ausf. C* towing a *5-cm PaK 38* antitank gun. The half-track was well suited to the desert environment and very much in demand as both an armored personnel carrier and tow vehicle.

An *Sd.Kfz. 251/6* armored command vehicle, issued to the headquarters staff of *Panzer* divisions and motorized units. The equiment carried included encoders, deciphering machines, and extensive radio equipment. The range of the radio was nominally fifty kilometers, but in the desert, with little high terrain to mask transmissions, the range was often considerably greater.

An *Sd.Kfz. 251 Ausf. C* with riveted construction towing a 5-cm *PaK 38.*

An armored half-track passes a very "Beau Geste"–type fort. The *Reich* war flag was used for air-recognition purposes.

British Mark II Matilda tanks on the move. British tank tactics were initially quite unimaginative. Desperately seeking out the *Panzers,* British tanks ran headlong into antitank gun screens and concealed *Panzers,* suffering heavy casualties in the process.

A knocked-out British Mark II Matilda tank, used primarily for infantry support. The Matilda was heavily armored but slow and mounted the inadequate 2-pounder gun. Only the 88 was capable of dealing with the Matilda at long range. The damage indicates an internal explosion of ammunition.

A destroyed Humber Mark III armored car mounting a 2-pounder main gun. A U.S.-made jeep is in the background. The two-color camouflage scheme is unusual on British vehicles.

Heinz Werner Schmidt: "I accompanied Rommel on a personal inspection of the battlefield along the frontier from Halfaya to Sidi Omar. We counted 180 knocked-out British tanks, mostly Mark II's."* The majority of these were destroyed by 8.8-cm antiaircraft guns used in the antitank role.

* Heinz Schmidt, *With Rommel in the Desert* (London, 1951), 51.

An Infantry Tank Mark II "Matilda," slow and armed only with a 2-pounder (40mm) main gun but well protected with armor up to 78mm. However, in this instance, the armor has been penetrated numerous times. A number of these hits seem to be from subcaliber rounds. This is possibly a destroyed vehicle set up as a target to test various antitank weapons. Of interest is the stenciled loading data that appears to be in German.

The American M3 Stuart was nicknamed the "Honey" by the British as it was extremely fast and maneuverable. It is seen here protecting soft-skin vehicles in a typical British "Leaguer" position.

Panzer II's and a *Panzer III* move across a broad expanse of open desert. For unknown reasons, the turret of the *Panzer III* is traversed to the rear.

An M3 Stuart light tank of American manufacture supplied to the British. The Stuart was fast and armed with a 37-mm main gun. It was intended as a reconnaissance/scout vehicle.

A captured M3 Stuart in service with the German forces. The Germans utilized a great deal of captured Allied equipment since their own was generally in short supply.

A destroyed M3 Stuart with a good bit of external stowage. This was necessary as the crew compartment was quite cramped.

Resupply for a *Panzer III Ausf. H* armed with the shorter 5.0-cm L/42 main gun. This weapon was capable of dealing with most of the Allied main battle tanks of this period, such as the Crusader. This *Panzer III* is from *Panzer-Regiment 8* of the *15. Panzer-Division*. The regimental affiliation can be determined by the tactical sign of the *15. Panzer-Division* on the left front of the vehicle (to the left of the driver's station).

An early-model *Panzer IV* with a short 7.5-centimeter main gun. This particular tank is the 3rd tank of the 1st Platoon of the 8th Company. It must be considered relatively early in the campaign, since this version of the *Panzer IV* was fast growing obsolete, with uparmored and upgunned versions of the *Panzer IV* appearing until the war's end, thus becoming the mainstay of the *Panzerwaffe* and the only tank that saw continuous service from the beginning to the end of the war.

An uparmored *Panzer II Ausf. C.* Note the additional armor applied to the gun mantlet. Additional 2.0-cm armor plates were applied to all A, B, and C models in 1940. This *Panzer* is from *Panzer-Regiment 5* of the *5. leichte Division* (later *21. Panzer-Division*).

A *Panzer III* moves at speed across the desert terrain with crewmembers and additional passengers riding outside the vehicle to beat the heat. The tank is passing a knocked-out or abandoned British-built Bofors antiaircraft gun.

The smoke from burning vehicles in the background indicates that a major battle has been fought. Two *Panzer II's* perform overwatch duties. The German soldier in the foreground may be from a communications unit.

Italian soldiers pass a command version of the *Panzer III*, a *Panzerbefehlswagen III*, which can be recognized by the large frame antenna on its rear deck. To accommodate the extra radios, the turret was fixed in place and the main gun removed, with a dummy gun mounted so as to help maintain the appearance of a regular tank.

A column of *Panzer III's* and *Sd.Kfz. 222* armored cars moves along what was considered to be a "main road" in North Africa. Given the mixed nature of the column, this might be an advance guard for a force.

Knocked-out vehicles give grim testimony to recent fighting.

Another view of a *Panzer III* moving at speed in the desert. Note the storage of the pith helmets on the outside of the turret, since there was little room in the fighting compartment for personal items.

The appearance of heavy French and English tanks during the French campaign prompted the Germans to come up with makeshift answers to combat the problem. One solution was the conversion of the obsolescent *Panzer I* into a tank destroyer by the removal of the turret and the mounting of a captured Czech 4.7-cm antitank gun. This tank destroyer was designated *4.7-cm PaK(t) auf Panzerkampfwagen 1 Ausf. B* and was the first of many tank destroyer designs to make use of obsolete tank chassis. 202 were converted from March 1940 to February 1941. This vehicle was probably assigned to *Panzerjäger-Bataillon 605*, a field-army troop unit used in direct support of subordinate forces.

A *Marder III (Sd.Kfz. 139)* self-propelled antitank gun. This tank destroyer was based on the chassis of the Skoda tank, the *Panzer 38(t)*, and featured a Soviet 7.62-centimeter antitank gun in a sheet-metal fighting compartment with limited traversing ability. These guns were assigned to *Panzerjäger-Abteilung 33 (15. Panzer-Division)* in North Africa. So efective was the high-velocity gun on this vehicle that the British thought the Germans had mounted an 88.

British tankers inspect a late-model *Panzer III*, which has been knocked out. The British tank is an A 13 Crusader.

This self-propelled artillery piece—a *15 cm s.I.G. 33 auf Fahrgestell Panzer II (Sf)*—was an extremely rare variant, having had a production run of only twelve. They were employed exclusively in North Africa and assigned to *schwere Infanterie-Geschütz-Kompanie (Sf) 707* and *708*. It must be viewed as an early attempt to provide German forces with self-propelled artillery. Since the tanks and other mechanized forces often outran the towed artillery, the advantages of a mechanized piece that required no unlimbering to set up are obvious. The gun mounted here was a 15-centimeter Model 33 heavy infantry gun.

Two excellent profile shots of *Panzer III's* mounting the 5.0-cm L/60 (above) and the lower-velocity L/42 (below).

SUPPLY BATTALION

The forces in the field sometimes took elaborate measures to remind them of their homeland when the time and opportunity presented itself. The 29035 is the field post number of the organization, which was the *2. große Kraftwagenkolonne, Nachschubkolonnenabteilung 553* (a truck section of the 553rd Supply Battalion).

The vehicles of the unit are unloaded at Tripoli.

Taking in the sights before deployment to the far less hospitable desert battlefield.

Unfortunately, the subject of these photographs, and the compiler of the photo album, cannot be indentified.
Below: Comrades-in-arms. Two army soldiers pose with a *Luftwaffe* airman and Italian compatriots.

German and Italian soldiers enjoy a hand of cards in a staging area.

The supply vehicles with their essential supplies move out. In the absence of railways across most of North Africa, all supplies were transported by trucks directly from the docks to the fighting units.

These soldiers have just received the Iron Cross, Second Class.

This soldier has just been awarded the War Service Cross, Second Class. In addition, he wears a sports badge and what appears to be an East medal ribbon. If so, then he was probably part of the *10. Panzer-Division*, which was transferred to North Africa in late 1942 from the Eastern Front.

A marble arch—the Arco dei Fieini—constructed by Italian forces from the days of colonization marks the border between Tripolitania and Cyrenaica. It was the scene of frequent photographs, since it stood out so boldly against the stark desert landscape.

A supply depot or way station next to a major road. The buildings are prefabricated and easily assembled.

Loading up at a major supply dump situated in a substantial fort.

Camouflaged shelter halves have been used to erect a rather elaborate tent. Note the flag on the staff, perhaps denoting this was the commander's tent or the tentage served as a command post.

Soldiers enjoy a meal in the field in relative comfort—that is, if you discount the ever-present flies that landed on every scrap of exposed food and would not move even when attempts were made to brush them off.

The supply section poses for a group photo. The officer in command can be seen on the viewer's far left. Although officer insignia cannot be detected, the round belt buckle was used exclusively by officers, with the enlisted personnel wearing rectangular ones.

Soldiers use a break in the fighting to socialize around a camp stove.

Supply trucks are staged for a run to the front.

A soldier strikes a warlike pose in a captured Bren carrier from the British 1st Armoured Division, dating this image to sometime after November 1941, when the division was first sent to North Africa.

It was rare to have any female company in the desert. Surrounded by admiring Italian and German soldiers, the young lady may be a member of an entertainment troupe, as might the gentleman in civilian clothes on the far left.

Rations are distributed to runners from various sections, who each hold a number of mess tins.

The coastal highway was the only major paved road in North Africa. As such, it was a vital supply line for both sides and subject to intensive interdiction from both air forces.

A captured British Chevrolet supply truck with prominent *Balkenkreuz* identification. A considerable part of the German supply columns consisted of captured British trucks.

THE LUFTWAFFE AND REGIA AERONAUTICA

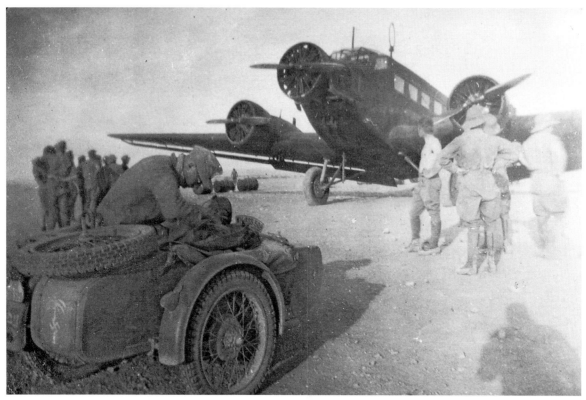

A tri-motor *Junkers Ju 52* transport aircraft has landed in the desert to resupply forward forces, as evidenced by the fuel drums in the background. Rommel's lead forces frequently outstripped the ability of the ground logistical network to keep up with them.

A *Feiseler Fi 156 Storch* (Stork) liason aircraft, known for its phenomenal short take-off and landing capabilities.

A *Junkers Ju 52* transport on a resupply mission. Note how low the aircraft is to the water. Most flights were made at this altitude in order to both avoid detection and make fighter attacks more difficult.

A *Dornier Do 17Z* bomber after a crash-landing. The *Do 17* was also often used as a reconnaissance aircraft.

A *Ju 87R Stuka* that appears to still be painted in its 70/71/65 dark green/blue European-theater camouflage. As the Allied air forces did not gain complete air superiority until late 1942, the *Ju 87* was a highly effective ground-support aircraft until then.

This series of photographs depicts a *Ju 87 Stuka* entering its almost vertical dive. The Stuka was able to deliver its bomb load with incredible precision.

A wrecked *Ju 87 Stuka*, possibly a later D model, either being cannibalized for spares or searched for souvenirs.

A *Bf 110C* heavy fighter and a *Ju 88* bomber share an advance airfield. Adequate *Luftwaffe* support was crucial for the success of the *Afrikakorps*. The much-maligned 110 performed very well in the desert skies.

The
COLOR
of WAR

Enlisted Man's Tropical Field Blouse Made of Cotton Twill

Campaign Cuff Title Introduced in January 1943

Deutsches Afrikakorps Cuff Title Introduced in July 1941

Belt Buckle with Canvas Belt

Second Pattern Tropical Breeches

Tropical Shorts in Olive-colored Cotton Twill

Tropical Straight-Leg Pants Made of Cotton Twill

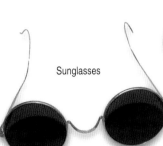

Sunglasses

Tropical Dust Glasses

Tropical Field Blouse,
Reconnaissance Unit,
with Afrikakorps Cuff Title,
Ribbon for Iron Cross,
2nd Class; and Infantry
Assault Badge

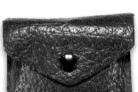

Sun/Dust Goggles

Non-Standard North
African Sun Helmet
Made of Wicker

First-Pattern Tropical Pith Helmet

Second-Pattern Tropical Pith Helmet

Army Steel Helmet
in Dark Yellow Paint

Enlisted Man's
M40 Tropical
Field Cap

Panzer Enlisted
Man's Tropical
Overseas Cap

Tropical Combat Rucksack

Flashlight with Color Filters

M31 Tropical Canteen Made of Aluminum with Plastic Impregnated Wood Cover and Cup

M1931 Bread Bag

Afrika Korps Ring. (These rings were hand-crafted and not official issue.)

Italian/German African Campaign Medal— Awarded Only to German Military Personnel

Leather Marching Boots

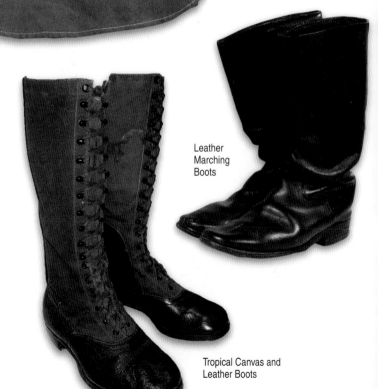

PANZERGRUPPE AFRIKA

Kalender 1942

Soldier's Notebook/Journal

Soldbuch

Soldier's Pay and Record Book

Tropical Canvas and Leather Boots

M1931
Mess Kit

Tropical Canvas
Webbing Straps

MG 34/42
Ammunition Drum

M35 Map/Dispatch
Case

Gear and Webbing
Harness Typically Worn
by Infantry Soldiers

MG-34 Machine Gun with 7.92 x 57mm
Ammunition Belt and Case

Soldier's Personal Items

THE WEHRMACHT

KAR98k Bolt-Action Rifle 7.92mm

Bayonet and Five-Round Ammunition Clips

P08 Luger

P38 Walther 9mm

Walther 7.65mm PPK

MP40 with Magazine Pouch and Luger Holster

KAR98k Ammunition Pouch

Entrenching Tool

M1928 Stick Grenade

Gas Mask Canister

Kingdom of Italy Flag

Tropical Field Cap

M35 Leather
Tanker Helmet

64th Infantry
Division Catanzaro
Lieutenant's
Uniform

Carcano M38 Rifle, 7.35mm Caliber

Moschetto Automatico Beretta Modello
1938 9mm Submachine Gun

Beretta M1935
Semi-Automatic
Pistol, .32 Caliber

THE ITALIAN ARMY

M33 Combat Helmet in North African Paint Scheme

Tropical Pith Helmet

M33 Combat Helmet in European Paint Scheme

Bersaglieri Pith Helmet

Tropical Breeches

Tropical Short Pants

A tri-motor SM 82 transport used to ferry *Afrikakorps* soldiers to North Africa.

Refuelling at an advance airfield. A *Ju 87 Stuka* is in the background.

An Italian Caproni Ca 311 makes a landing approach.

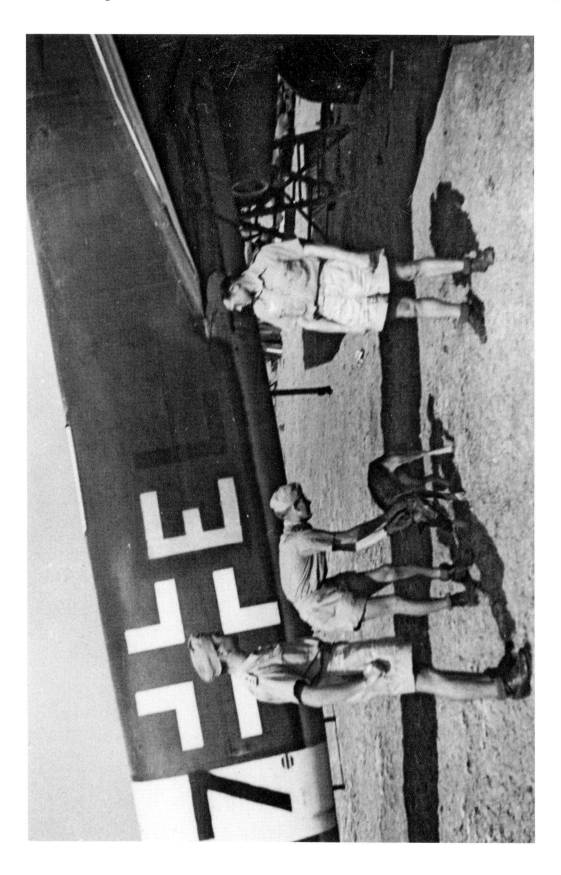

A series of photographs of *I Gruppe, Kampfgeschwader 54 "Totenkopf,"* equipped with the superb *Junkers Ju 88* bomber.

Fitting long-range drop tanks to the external bomb racks.

Above and next two pages: *SC-250 Minenbombe* of approximately 550 pounds. This type along with the *SC-500* was standard *Luftwffe* ordnance for bombers. Without their arming fuses, the bombs are relatively inert. Two of the unit's *Ju 88's* are in the background.

A celebration on the completion of 100 missions. There was no official limit on the number of missions aircrew flew. The idea of a maximum of 25 or 50 missions, as was the case with Allied aircrews, was regarded with astonishment by *Luftwaffe* crews.

SC-50 Minenbombe, fitted with "Jericho Trumpets" on the tail fins. These devices made a loud whistling sound as the bombs fell in order to futher unsettle the enemy.

A *Fi 156 Fieseler Storch* light utility aircraft. These aircraft were frequently used for observation purposes and often dropped messages to commanders on the ground. The "Stork" was used throughout the war for this and many other purposes, including the evacuation of wounded from the battlefield. This aircraft had exceptional short takeoff and landing capabilities. Senior *Afrikakorps* commanders, including Rommel, used it frequently. Rommel was in the habit of "dropping in" on tardy or lost formations and getting them moving in the right direction.

A Fiat G50 bis and a *Messerschmitt Bf 110C* fly in formation. The Italian fighter pilots were generally very skillful at aerobatics and liked to dogfight. The *Luftwaffe* pilots were more aggressive and preferred, with the advantage of altitude, to dive on an opponent and shoot them down in a single pass. If they were not successful, they attempted to gain altitude again and repeat the tactic.

ROMMEL

Rommel, the "Desert Fox," having just been awarded the German-Italian Campaign Medal. Bold, impetuous, and hard-driving, he was a brilliant tactician who was not only a master of offensive operations but also most adept at defensive tactics when these were required. Rommel was tough on his troops, expecting almost superhuman efforts, but equally unsparing of himself, sharing the hazards of the battlefield with the common soldier. However, his relationships with subordinate and superior officers was not always harmonious.

The fast-moving, constantly changing battles in North Africa suited Rommel's direct and fluid command style far better than his British contemporaries. Rommel was able to adapt his plans instantly to current circumstances in contrast to the more pedestrian British generals. Here Rommel confers with one of his regimental commanders.

Rommel, always at or near the front, studies a map with what appears to be an aide (viewer's left) and a field-grade officer who has seen First World War service (as indicated by the Iron Cross, First Class, on his breast pocket).

The "Desert Fox" in a characteristic pose, standing in one of his staff cars while on an inspection tour of the front. The cap seen in this picture was taken from Rommel's estate in Germany by a U.S. soldier and is currently on display at a museum in Texas.

Rommel in a candid photo taken by a soldier in the field.

General Sir Claude Auchinleck, the Middle East theater commander, said this of his opponent Rommel: "There is a real danger that our friend Rommel is becoming a kind of bogey-man to our troops, who are talking far too much about him. He is by no means a superman, although he is very energetic and able. Even if he were a superman, it would still be highly undesirable that our men should credit him with superhuman powers. I wish to dispel by all possible means that Rommel represents something more than an ordinary German general, quite an unpleasant one though, as we have heard from his own officers."[*]

[*] Richard Law and Craig W. H. Luther, *Rommel* (San Jose, 1980), 47.

Rommel confers with a group of commanders from a medium cross-country personnel car.

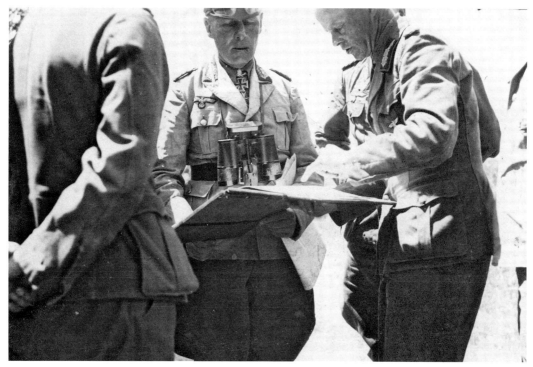

Rommel wearing his Knight's Cross with Oak Leaves and Swords as well as his *Pour le Mérite* (Blue Max). This photograph was taken late in the campaign as evident from his gaunt look and the strain of constant battle on his face.

Rommel with *General der Panzertruppe* Walter Nehring.

The orders conference has concluded (see photo on the bottom of page 102) and the relentless Rommel moves on to the next one. Sometimes Rommel took these front-line forays too far and was away from his headquarters at critical times. However, his uncanny ability to sense enemy intentions and act quickly to counter them was one of his greatest strengths.

ARTILLERY

A *Luftwaffe* gun crew with their *2-cm Flak 30.*

A demonstration firing of a quad *2-cm Flak 38*, as evidenced by the presence of a cameraman along the outer edge of the photograph. A very effective weapon in both the antiaircraft and ground roles.

Luftwaffe airmen observe as a technician makes adjustments to a gun cradle on a 2-centimeter *Flak 152*. The divisions in Africa generally had a *Flak* battalion in direct support of them for area and point defense. This particular weapon has apparently seen lots of action, as denoted by the numerous "kill" rings on its barrel. These were not necessarily aircraft "kills," as the *Flak* were often employed in direct-fire ground support roles as well.

An *leFH 18 10-5-cm* howitzer being unloaded at the port of Tripoli or Benghazi. Note the "dazzle" camouflage on the transport that was intended to disrupt the aim of submarines.

A *leichte Feld-Haubitze 18 (leFH 18)* and gun crew prepare to fire over open sights. This was the standard light field piece of the divisional artillery, and each regiment usually had two battalions of eighteen guns each. In this case, crewmembers attempt to hold down in the gun trails in preparation for firing. Given the evidence of a hasty firing, there was probably no time to dig in. All of the men wear the iconic M40 tropical billed field cap, which appears to have been bleached almost white, either by prolonged exposure to the intense African sun or artificially by means of some bleaching agent, which many soldiers in North Africa did in order to achieve an instant "vet" appearance.

The standard German antitank gun going into the campaign in North Africa was the 3.7-centimeter *PaK 36*. It soon proved to be as inadequate there as it was in France, but it continued to be used until replacement antitank guns of larger caliber could be fielded. A crew poses with its weapon in this image.

The formidable 7.5-cm *PaK 40* antitank gun being towed by a *Sd.Kfz 10* half-track. The *PaK 40* was capable of dealing with any Allied tank, including the M4 Sherman, at long range.

An 8.8-cm *Flak 18* with its *Sd.Kfz. 7* towing vehicle. The *Flak 18* weighed seven tons in travelling order. The half-track carried the gun crew of eleven men.

A 5-cm *PaK 38* antitank gun and crew member. A very effective high-velocity weapon capable of dealing with all Allied tanks at medium to short ranges of 500 to 1,000 meters. It replaced the puny 3.7-cm *PaK 36* from late 1940 onward.

An 88 being limbered after action. The large size of the crew (eleven) needed to operate this formidable weapon is evident.

The *8.8-cm Flak 18*, the famous 88, here in use in the antiaircraft role. Note the sandbag protection and the gun shield, allowing this deadly weapon to be used in the antitank role.

LIFE IN THE DESERT

Rommel stands by as General Garibaldi addresses some of his senior commanders. Although Rommel garnered all the headlines, Garibaldi was the official commander in chief in North Africa. Rommel's relationships with Garibaldi and most of the Italian high command were generally very acrimonious. In fact, Rommel and Garibaldi almost came to blows on one occasion.

Soldiers preparing individual positions in the hard desert floor.

A motorcycle messenger poses with his "ride," a 750 cc BMW R75. Of interest is the ubiquitous *Afrikakorps* insignia—a palm tree with a superimposed swastika—on the sidecar. Note also the presence of a blackout cover for the vehicle's headlight.

Fresh fruit and vegetables were a luxury in the desert. It is not evident if these delicacies were procured from the local populace or "liberated" from a British supply column. German rations were usually inadequate, as Rommel's aide Heinz Werner Schmidt explained to General Paulus: "Fruit and vegetables are unknown to the soldier. They miss their potatoes especially. The rations consist of sardines in oil, bulky tinned-meat sausages (*Bierwurst*), and 'Alter Mann.' The small round tins of tough beef were all marked A.M. . . . The men declared that this stood for 'Alter Mann' or 'Old Man.'"*

* Heinz Schmdt, *With Rommel in the Desert* (London, 1951), 47.

The Volkswagen *Kübelwagen* ("bucket vehicle") was the standard German staff car of World War II. The soldiers wear the early campaign headgear, a pith helmet modeled on British and Dutch designs. It was almost universally replaced by the billed field cap—the M40—soon after deployment to the African continent. These soldiers appear to be in the process of acclimating to the new theater of operations.

The tedious task of "digging in," with so little natural cover available, was essential to survival.

Enlisted soldiers take time for cold rations in their *Kübelwagen*. As evidenced by the wearing of greatcoats, the desert was an environment of changing temperatures.

German soldiers take a break from the fighting to recreate the capture of a British soldier for the camera.

A touch of civilized living in a harsh environment.

A soldier undergoes a dentist's inspection in the field. Intervals in the fighting were used to catch up on important personnel issues such as these. The white crosses on the "Jerry" cans indicate they were filled with potable water.

A field grave for *Unteroffizier* Andres, who was assigned to a machine-gun battalion. It was typical earlier in the war for German forces to mark field gravesites with the headgear of the fallen.

The "Ship of the Desert," useful for hauling supplies to difficult-to-reach locations.

A break in the fighting is used to hold a grenade-throwing contest. The long handle of the German "Potato Masher" grenade enabled it to be thrown a longer distance, and usually more accurately, than the Allied equivalent.

A seasoned *Afrikakorps* veteran, judging by his impressive tan. The makeshift nature of his accommodation is obvious. In the background is the ubiquitous "Jerry Can" that the Allies quickly adopted. Initally, the British stored their ready supplies of gasoline and water in flimsy tins that frequently split and leaked.

Plotting a route through the largely featureless terrain took a great deal of skill. Axis and Allied units frequently became lost, both on the march and even during combat operations.

An interesting portrait of a tanker in tropical uniform, who is wearing the traditional *Totenkopf* ("Death's Head") insignia on his collar in lieu of the standard tropical braid. He appears to be wearing white denim work trousers as opposed to "true" tropical trousers, which were brown in color. Given the background, this soldier may also have been in Greece at the time of this photograph and a member of the *1. Panzer-Division*, which was sent to the Mediterranean country from Russia in 1943 for reconstitution and whose personnel were known to have worn tropical uniforms with this insignia variation.

A close-up view of the same *Panzer* soldier on the previous page.

A very nice studio portrait of a tropical soldier who has been awarded the German-Italian Campaign Medal. This was normally worn as a ribbon, but the awardee was allowed to wear the medal on the first day of its award. He is wearing the first-pattern tropical field tunic and a later (or modified) sun-bleached M40 tropical billed field cap (lack of branch-of-service color).

A very fine portrait of an *Afrika Korps Gefreiter* (corporal) in full regulation uniform, including the much-disliked pith helmet.

A machine-gun outpost at the ready. These soldiers appear to be members of the *Hermann Göring* division, elements of which were hastily flown in late in the campaign to bolster the sagging German fortunes in that theater of war. Both the gunner and his assistant appear to be wearing SS-pattern camouflage smocks, which is a means of identifying this division, since it was the only formation in theater that would have worn that uniform item. Interestingly enough, however, the men all appear to be wearing army versions of the M40 tropical billed field cap, which makes identifying this photograph with complete accuracy difficult. The machine gun appears to be an *MG 15*.

A machine-gun position with the very effective *MG34*, a far superior weapon to anything the British could field. The Vickers machine gun was reliable but cumbersome as it was water-cooled. The rocky nature of the ground made it difficult to dig in.

On watch. Another machine-gun position, this time in terrain more suitable for digging trenches.

This page and the next: *Afrikakorps* soldiers relax on a *3.7-cm PaK 36.* They are wearing the canvas and leather lace-up tropical boot which was specifically designed for use in North Africa. This was a non-drying boot, meaning that the harsh environment would not cause the material to dry out and crack. There was also an ankle-length model of this popular boot.

Rommel's headquarters at Agedabia. Field-telephone lines are evident.

Time for a quick meal before returning to duty. Captured British rations were much preferred over German and Italian fare, which included tins of sardines that went rancid and tubes of cheese that became liquid.

Mealtime in the desert. The standard aluminum mess tin is being used as a cook pot. Allied canned goods were far superior to the German and Italian variety—and highly prized.

Provided there was no interference from the Royal Navy or Air Force, the sea voyage to Africa could be enjoyable.

A group of *Luftwaffe* pilots, two of whom have been awarded the Knight's Cross.

This page and the next: Two excellent photographs of expedient field accommodations of a semi-permanent nature. In the desert, improvisation was essential.

Establishing a field-telephone connection. Unlike radio transmissions, messages could not be intercepted unless the line was directly tapped into.

Due to the good condition of the uniforms and less than battle-ready appearance, these soldiers are probably rear-echelon personnel. German combat units generally had a substantailly smaller logistical component than equivalent Allied units.

A group of *Afrika Korps* soldiers in full tropical kit, including knee-length canvas/leather tropical boots and the very popular tropical visored field cap.

A memento for the family at home. The soldier's awards include the Iron Cross, Second Class; Wound Badge; and possibly the General Assault Badge.

Another excellent portrait shot of an *Afrika Korps Panzer Schütze*. Note the death's head insignia on the collar of the field blouse. *Panzer* troops were authorized to wear the insignia in this manner. The breeches and knee boots are also evident.

This impressively decorated officer's medals include the Wound Badge (probably in black), Infantry Assault Badge, DRL Sports Badge, and what appears to be an Honor Roll Clasp.

An *MG 34* set up in the antiaircraft role. Note the prominent ring sight.

An unidentified *Hauptmann* (captain) poses in front of a German military cemetery. The marker reads: "To Our Fallen Heroes."

The same *Hauptmann* seen in the previous photo outside a medical clearing facility. A *Kübelwagen* and a *Kfz. 11* are in the background.

A substantial fortification that has seen some heavy action. Fortifications such as these were positioned at numerous strategic points in the desert. Despite the age of some of these structures, they often proved to be formidable defensive positions.

The most important commodity in the desert: water. A half-track and trucks being supplied from a substantial well. The white cross on the "Jerry Cans" indicates they contain water.

Every soldier knows that when the opportunity presents itself, you try to get some sleep.

Judging by the tricolor flag, this is an Italian military cemetery.

A *Hauptmann* operates an Enigma device, which was used to encrypt and decrypt classified messages. Unbeknownst to the Germans, the Polish had cracked the code in 1932 and presented their knowledge of the system to British and French intelligence in the summer of 1939. Consequently, almost all major military traffic the Germans sent was capable of being decoded, thus immeasurably aiding the Allied war effort.

Below: A field switchboard in operation. The Germans probably made more use of wire communications than any other combatant in World War II.

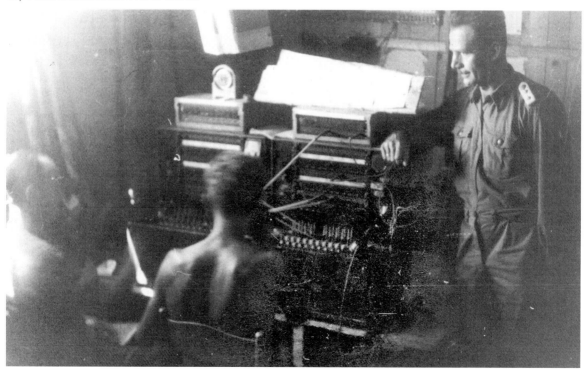

An *Oberst* (colonel) enjoys very comfortable quarters with floor coverings and even a wash basin. Given the constant movement of the combat units, this is most likely a semi-permanent rear-area encampment.

A conference beside a captured British truck.

Catching up on some sleep near Mameli.

Two light cross-country personnel cars negotiate a desert track. Vehicles like these were often used for reconnaissance purposes although armored cars were more suitable.

Italian troops on parade in a major city, possibly Tripoli. Many disparaging things have been written about the combat performance of the Italians. However, when properly led and supplied with proper equipment, they fought bravely and well. At the second battle of El Alamein, several Italian units doggedly defended their positions until they were wiped out.

Two Carro Armato light tanks stand guard. The frontal armor was a reasonable 40mm and the main gun was 20mm.

Supplies being unloaded outside Marsa Matruh on 11 July 1942. Marsa Matruh was the scene of a major defeat for the British 8th Army in late June 1942 that led to their retreat to El Alamein. In the foreground is a Type 82 *Kübelwagen*.

An interesting image of a *Luftwaffe Feldwebel* (sergeant) who continues to wear his "continental" visor cap in North Africa.

A *Kfz. 12 Horch* medium cross-country personnel vehicle, one of the most widely used early-war vehicles of this type. These types of vehicles were considered too complicated and costly for wartime production and were phased out in 1941, to be replaced by the Type 82 *Kübelwagen*.

On watch from a desert escarpment. The flat, monotonous desert was only rarely broken by high ground such as this, which was highly prized and often bitterly contested, such as at the battle for Halfaya Pass in June 1941 by the 4th Indian Division as part of Operation "Battleaxe." This was Wavell's last attempt to eject Rommel from Cyrenaica and relieve the garrison at Tobruk.

Precious fuel being protected from the heat. Fuel was Rommel's major supply bottleneck, and a lack of fuel hampered the operational freedom that was essential in the desert. British naval units and torpedo-bombers from Malta specifically targeted fuel tankers, as did the *Luftwaffe* when attacking the vital Malta convoys.

Permanent buildings were almost non-existent outside the major towns. This is a communications center.

Most soldiers had to make do with small two-man tents.

British/Commonwealth prisoners guarded by Italian soldiers. The treatment of prisoners by both sides was humane and in line with the Geneva Convention. One exception was the treatment of prisoners by the Vichy French forces in Syria and Algeria, which was often very harsh.

An elaborate German and Italian military cemetery.

This page and the top of the next: The Germans were most respectful of their war dead and made every effort to bury the fallen with dignity. Where possible, each grave was marked with the name of the fallen and the date. Both sides respected these grave sites.

Tents very well protected by an impressive stone wall. This may be part of the siege ring around Tobruk.

The town of Derna. The large sign states that it is forbidden to find your own quarters—all quarters must be officially allocated.

Two contrasting views of a desert campsite. Above, the somewhat elaborate set-up looks to be semi-permanent. Stones have even been laid to delineate the path. Below, the situation could not be more different. A tarpaulin has been stretched between three poles and a box used as a table.

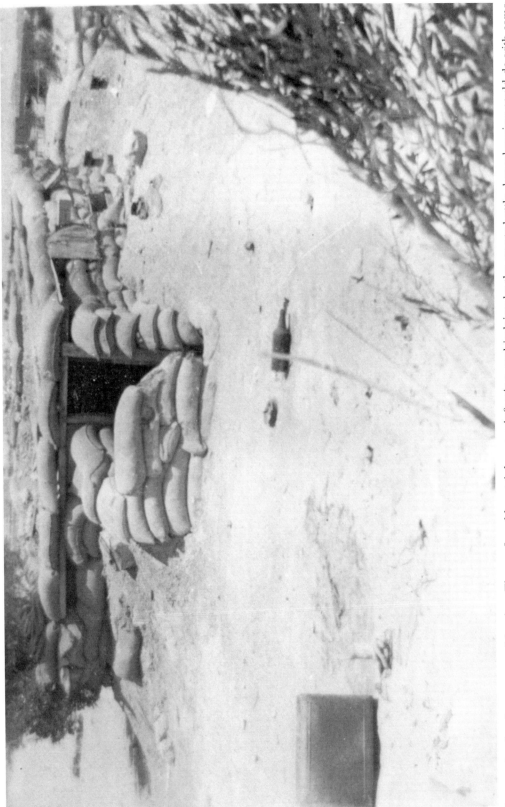

A somewhat hastily constructed bunker. The roof could certainly use reinforcing, and judging by the empty bottle, housekeeping could do with some improvement also.

An ammunition dump of heavy artilley shells. Quite possibly, this position has been recently captured.

A very elaborate amphitheater constructed for some special ceremony or celebration.

This is most likely a street scene in Tripoli. Major towns were rare in North Africa and usually centered on ports such as Tripoli, Benghazi, and Tobruk.

The elaborate architecture identifies this town as Tripoli, the major supply base for the *Afrikakorps*. Tripoli possessed an excellent deep-water port but was hundreds of miles away from the front lines. The long supply lines limited the operations of both sides. The farther they advanced, the longer and more tenuous the suppy lines became.

Two views of a desert encampment. Roasting hot during the day and freezing cold at night.

TRANSPORT VEHICLES

A wheeled field ambulance is offloaded from its cargo transporter.

A *Luftwaffe Unteroffizier* (sergeant) supervises the work of an airman maintaining a truck.

A light cross-country personnel car with an unusual camouflaged soft top.

A captured British supply truck. The *Afrikakorps* made wide use of captured British vehicles

A *Kfz. 11* medium cross-country personnel carrier. This vehicle has been well fitted for desert operations.

An Italian truck driver poses in front of his heavy truck of Italian manufacture. Italian units were not equipped with anywhere near adequate motor transport, making troop movements and supply very difficult.

A medium cross-country personnel carrier and crew.

The same type of vehicle as in the previous photograph, with a crew member striking a suitably heroic pose. Note the Iron Cross, Second Class, ribbon and the Infantry Assault Badge.

This page and top next: Outside the fortress of Tobruk, June 1941. The tactical symbol appears to be for a motorized machine-gun company.

Maintenance was essential if you were to survive in the desert. To some extent, all vehicle crews had to be their own mechanics. The truck is an Opel Model 3.6.

At work on a captured British Ford WOT2H truck. The *Afrikakorps* never had enough vehicles and relied heavily on captured British vehicles to maintain mobility.

Working on the front suspension and the brakes. The wide variety of vehicles used by both sides and the lack of spare parts taxed the maintenance sections to the limit of their abilities.

The crew of a light communications truck take a break.

The same communications unit featured on the previous page takes time to pose for photographs. German troops were well supplied with excellent compact 35mm cameras from companies such as Robot. Photographs by anyone other than official photographers were forbidden for security reasons. This ruling was by and large ignored.

The same unit makes camp. If they are on radio-intercept duties in a forward area, they could spend several days in this position. A telegraph pole is in the background, so the unit could also be either establishing communications or tapping the wire.

This supply truck sports a unique camouflage pattern.

Setting off on a reconnaissance mission in a light cross-country personnel vehicle.

A heavy cross-country personnel car (six-passenger) *Kfz. 21* on the standard medium armored car chassis. The Germans made far too many specialized vehicles with not enough standardization of chassis, engines, or parts. Add to this the widespread use of captured equipment and keeping all these vehicles maintained and operational became a logistical nightmare.

Supply missions were carried out over long distances of up to 1,000 miles from Tripoli to the front lines. The trip was both tedious and dangerous. The Allied air forces—British, Australian, and South African—operated by both day and night to interdict these operations.

A soldier enjoys the relatively rare luxury of a field bath.

In addition to the many other logistical requirements of an army in the field, the trucking of potable water was also a vital necessity in the harsh desert climate.

Refuelling in progress at Rommel's headquarters near Agedabia.

A brief pause in Benghazi before heading to the front.

A captured British Ford WOT2H truck. The perforated steel plates on the sides of the truck are used for traction in deep sand.

APPENDIX A

Rank Comparisons

U.S. ARMY	BRITISH ARMY	GERMAN ARMY	ITALIAN ARMY
Enlisted Men			
Private	Private	*Schütze*	*Soldato*
Private First Class	Private 1st Class	*Oberschütze*	
Corporal	Lance Corporal	*Gefreiter*	*Caporale*
Senior Corporal	Corporal	*Obergefreiter*	*Caporal Maggiore*
Staff Corporal		*Stabsgefreiter*	
Noncommissioned Officers			
Sergeant	Sergeant	*Unteroffizier*	*Sergente*
	Staff Sergeant	*Unterfeldwebel*	
Staff Sergeant	Technical Sergeant	*Feldwebel*	
Sergeant First Class		*Oberfeldwebel*	
Master Sergeant	Master Sergeant	*Hauptfeldwebel*	
Sergeant Major	Sergeant Major	*Stabsfeldwebel*	*Sergente Maggiore*
Officers			
Second Lieutenant	Second Lieutenant	*Leutnant*	*Sotto Tenente*
First Lieutenant	First Lieutenant	*Oberleutnant*	*Tenente*
Captain	Captain	*Hauptman*	*Capitano*
Major	Major	*Major*	*Maggiore*
Lieutenant Colonel	Lieutenant Colonel	*Oberst Leutnant*	*Tenente Colonnello*
Colonel	Colonel	*Oberst*	*Colonnello*
Brigadier General	Brigadier General	*Generalmajor*	*Brigadier Generale*
Major General	Major General	*Generalleutnant*	*Maggiore Generale*
Lieutenant General	Lieutenant General	*General der Fallschirmjäger, etc.*	*Tenente Generale*
General	General	*Generaloberst*	*Generale*
General of the Army	Field Marshal	*Feldmarschall*	*Maresciallo d'Italia*

APPENDIX B

The *Afrika-Korps* Order of Battle in North Africa February 1941– October 1942

5. leichte Division

Arrived in Tripoli 14 February 1941. Reinforced, reorganized, and renamed as the *21. Panzer-Division* on 1 October 1941.

Commanders:

Generalmajor Johannes Streich, 20 February 1941–22 July 1941.

Generalmajor Johann von Ravenstein, 23 July 1941–1 October 1941.

Main Combat Formations:

Panzer-Regiment 5

1./Panzerjäger-Abteilung (mot)[1] 33

Panzerjäger-Abteilung (mot)[2] 39

Machinengewehr-Bataillon (mot) 2

Machinengewehr-Bataillon (mot) 8

I./Artillerie-Regiment (mot) 75

Flak-Abteilung (mot) 605

Flak-Abteilung (mot) 606

Aufklärungs-Abteilung[3] (mot) 3

1./Pionier-Bataillon[4] (mot) 39

15. Panzer-Division

Parts of the division arrived in Africa in late April 1941. By the middle of June, the division had completed its transfer.

Commanders:

Initial commander: *Generalmajor* Heinrich von Prittwitz, 22 March 1941–10 April 1941.

Final commander: *Oberst* Willibald Boroweitz, 12 December 1943–13 May 1943.

Main Combat Formations:

Panzer-Regiment 8

Panzerjäger-Abteilung (mot) 33

---

1. *(mot)* = motorized.

2. *Panzerjäger* = antitank.

3. *Aufklärungs* = reconnaissance.

4. *Pionier* = engineer.

Schützen-Brigade (mot) 15

       Infanterie-Regiment (mot) 115

       Infanterie-Regiment (mot) 200

       Maschinengewehr-Bataillon (mot) 8

       Kradschützen-Bataillon (mot) 15

Artillerie-Regiment (mot) 33

Aufklärungs-Abteilung (mot) 33

Pionier-Bataillon (mot) 33

Kradschützen-Bataillon (mot)(mot) 15

Artillerie-Regiment (mot) 33

Aufklärungs-Abteilung (mot) 33

Pionier-Bataillon (mot) 33

21. Panzer-Division

Formed from the *5. leichte Division* on 1 October 1941 in a considerably strengthened state.

Commanders:

Initial commander: *Generalmajor* Johann von Ravenstein, 1 October 1941–29 November 1941.

Final commander: *Generalmajor* Heinrich-Hermann von Hülsen, 25 April 1943–13 May 1943.

Main Combat Formations:

Panzer-Regiment 5

Panzerjäger-Abteilung (mot) 39

Infanterie-Regiment (mot) 104

Artillerie-Regiment (mot) 155

Aufklärungs-Abteilung (mot) 3

Pionier-Bataillon (mot) 200

90. leichte Afrika-Division

This division was initially designated as *Afrika-Division z.b.V.*[5] in August 1941. In March 1942, the division was reinforced and reorganized as *90. leichte Afrika-Division*.

Commanders:

Initial commander: *Generalmajor* Max Sümmermann, 17 July 1941–10 December 1941.

Final commander: *Generalleutnant* Theodor Graf von Sponek, 22 September 1942–12 May 1943.

Main Combat Formations:

Panzerjäger-Abteilung (mot) 190

Infanterie-Regiment (mot) 155

Infanterie-Regiment (mot) 200

Panzergrenadier-Regiment[6] *(mot) Afrika*

Kolbeck-Bataillon

Artillerie-Regiment (mot) 190

---

5. *z.b.V.* = for special duties.

6. *Panzergrenadier* = armored infantry.

schwerste Infanteriegeschütze-Kompanie[7] *707*

schwerste Infanteriegeschütze-Kompanie 708

Aufklärungs-Kompanie (mot) 580

Pionier-Bataillon (mot) 900

164. leichte Afrika-Division

Arrived in Africa in July 1942 from Crete.

Commanders:

Initial commander: *Oberst* Carl-Hans Lungerhausen, ? August 1942–31 August 1942.

Final commander: *Generalmajor* Kurt Freiherr von Liebenstein, 13 March 1943–13 May 1943.

Main Combat Formations:

Panzergrenadier-Regiment (mot) 125

Panzergrenadier-Regiment (mot) 382

Panzergrenadier-Regiment (mot) 433

Artillerie-Regiment (mot) 220

schwerste Infanteriegeschütze-Kompanie 707[8]

schwerste Infanteriegeschütze-Kompanie 708

Flak-Abteilung (mot) 609

Aufklärungs-Abteilung (mot) 220

Pionier-Bataillon (mot) 220

Fallschirm-Brigade Ramcke

The brigade completed its arrival in Africa by 17 August 1942 and was officially placed under the command of *Panzerarmee Afrika*. Positioned on the southern part of the Alamein front, the brigade was presumed destroyed when the front collapsed on 3 November 1942. However, the indefatigable Ramcke and his tough paratoopers captured a complete British supply column for an armored division. The now fully motorized *Brigade Ramcke* successfully completed a 200-mile trek through enemy territory, much to the astonishment of Rommel.

Commander:

Generalmajor Bernhard Ramcke, 16 July 1942–November 1942.

Major von der Heydte, November 1942–12 May 1943.

Main Combat Formations:

On its arrival in Africa, the brigade consisted of three *Jäger-Bataillone*, one *Panzerjäger-Kompanie*, one *Artillerie-Abteilung*, and one *Pionier-Kompanie*. The brigade had no organic transport capability and initially used the transport capacity of *Flak-Regiment 135*.

---

7. *schwerste Infanteriegeschütze-Kompanie* = heavy infantry gun (150mm) company.

8. Companies 707 and 708 transferred from the *90. leichte Afrika-Division* in August 1942.

APPENDIX C

Luftwaffe Units in Africa, October 1942

Fighter Units
Stab. JG 27 — Bf 109F and G
I/JG 27 — Bf 109F and G
II/ JG 27 — Bf 109F and G
III/JG 27 — Bf 109F and G
Jagdkommando Tobruk — Bf 109 F and G
II/JG 53 — Bf 109F and G
I/JG 77 — Bf 109F and G (In the process of deploying to Africa)
III/ZG 26 — Bf 110C

Ground-Attack
I/SG2 — Bf 109E

Tactical Reconnaissance
4(H)/12 — Bf 109E and F

Long-Range Reconnaissance
1(F)/121 — Ju 88
2(F)/123 — Ju 88

Bombers
III/KG 77 — Ju 88 (In the process of deploying to Africa)

Dive-Bombers
Stab. St.G 3 — Ju 87
I/St.G 3 — Ju 87
III/St.G 3 — Ju 87

SELECT BIBLIOGRAPHY

Agar-Hamilton, J., and L. Turner. *The Sidi Rezeg Battles 1941*. Capetown, 1957.

————. *Crisis in the Desert*. Capetown, 1952.

Barnett, Corelli. *The Desert Generals*. New York, 1961.

Bender, Roger, and Richard Law. *Uniforms, Organization and History of the Afrikakorps*. San Jose, 1973.

Law, Richard, and Craig W. H. Luther. *Rommel*. San Jose, 1980.

Carell, Paul. *The Foxes of the Desert*. New York, 1961.

Carver, Michael. *El Alamein*. New York, 1962.

————. *Tobruk*. Philadelphia, 1964.

Ciano, Count Galeazzo. *The Ciano Diaries, 1939–1943*. New York, 1946.

Chalfont, Alun. *Montgomery of Alamein*. London, 1976.

Churchill, Winston S. *The Second World War, Volume IV*. London, 1951.

Crisp, Robert. *Brazen Chariots*. London, 1966.

Dunning, Chris. *Combat Units of the Regia Aeronautica Italian Air Force, 1940–1943*. Oxford, 1988.

Fraser, David. *Knight's Cross: A Life of Field Marshall Erwin Rommel*. New York, 1993.

Griffith, Paddy. *World War II Desert Tactics*. Oxford, 2008.

Irving, David. *The Trail of the Fox*. London, 1977.

Jacobsen, H. and J. Rohwer. *Decisive Battles of World War II: The German View*. New York, 1965.

Kesselring, Albert. *Kesselring: A Soldier's Record*. New York, 1954.

Liddell Hart, Basil. *The German Generals Talk*. New York, 1948.

————. *The Rommel Papers*. New York, 1968.

————. *Liddell Hart's History of the Second World War*. London, 1973.

Luck, Colonel Hans von. *Panzer Commander*. New York, 1989.

Macksey, M. C. *Afrikakorps*. New York, 1968.

Massimello, Giovanni, and Giorgio Apostolo. *Italian Aces of World War 2*. Oxford, 2000.

Mellenthin, F. W. von. *Panzer Battles*. Harman, 1958.

Moorehead, Alan. *The Desert War*. London, 1965.

Pitt, Barrie. *The Crucible of War: Western Desert 1941*. London, 1980.

————. *The Crucible of War 2: Auchinleck's Command*. London, 1982.

————. *The Crucible of War 3: Montgomery and Alamein*. London, 1986.

Playfair, Ian. *The Mediterranean and the Middle East*.

————. *Volume 1: Early Successes against Italy*. London, 1954.

————. *Volume 2: The Germans Come to the Aid of Their Ally*. London, 1956.

————. *Volume 3: British Fortunes Reach Their Lowest Ebb*. London, 1960.

————. *Volume 4: The Destruction of Axis Forces in North Africa*. London, 1966.

Smith, J. Richard, and Martin Pegg. *Jagdwaffe, Volume 3, section 3, The War over the Desert, June 1940–June 1942*. Surrey, 2003.

Scheibert, Hans. *Deutscher Panzergrenadier 1939–1945*. Dorheim, 1966.

Scheibert, Hans, and C. Wagener. *Die Deutsche Panzertruppe 1939–1945*. Bad Nauheim, 1966.

Schmitt, Heinz. *With Rommel in the Desert*. London, 1951.

Shores, Christopher. *Luftwaffe Fighter Units Mediterranean 1941–1944*. London, 1978.

———. *Regia Aeronautica*, Vol. 1. Texas, 1976.

Shores, Christopher, and Hans Ring. *Fighters over the Desert*. New York, 1969.

Trevor-Roper, Hugh, ed. *Blitzkreig to Defeat*. New York, 1965.

———. *Hitler's War Directives 1939–1945*. London, 1966.

Warlimont, Walter. *Inside Hitler's Headquarters 1939–1945*. New York, 1964.

Weal, John. *Junkers Ju 87 Stukageschwader of North Africa and the Mediterranean*. London, 1998.

Young, Desmond. *Rommel—The Desert Fox*. New York, 1950.

ACKNOWLEDGMENTS

The following people deserve credit for their generous assistance in supplying period photographs taken by the combatants themselves, along with modern color images of uniforms, equipment, and weapons. In each and every case, they went above and beyond to help bring this book to life by offering their expertise and time: Pat Cassidy, Steve Cassidy, P. Whammond and Carey of Collector's Guild (www.germanmilitaria.com), Wilson History and Research Center (www.militaryheadgear.com), Jim Haley, David A. Jones, Jim Pool, Scott Pritchett, Phil Francis, and Aleks and Dmitri of Espenlaub Militaria (www.aboutww2militaria.com and www.warrelics.eu/forum), as well as the National Archives, the Swedish Army Museum, and a few individuals who wish to remain anonymous.

FURTHER READING FROM THE STACKPOLE MILITARY HISTORY SERIES

Now that you've seen the stark desert landscapes and the worn faces of the men who fought there, dig into the sand with the soldiers of the *Afrikakorps* in these vivid accounts of Rommel's war in North Africa. Here you'll find profiles of the officers who served under the Desert Fox, analyses of Rommel's leadership, descriptions of combat in the extremes of the desert, and stories from the other side. This is the desert war as it happened: Real Battles. Real Soldiers. Real Stories.

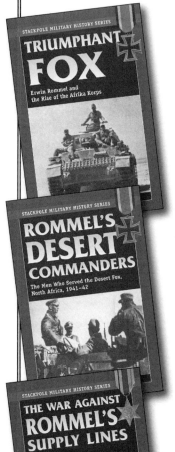

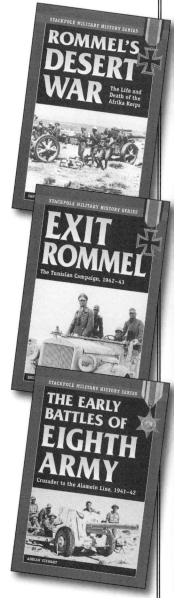

TRIUMPHANT FOX
Erwin Rommel and the Rise of the Afrika Korps
Samuel W. Mitcham Jr.
978-0-8117-3560-5

ROMMEL'S DESERT WAR
The Life and Death of the Afrika Korps
Samuel W. Mitcham Jr.
978-0-8117-3413-4

ROMMEL'S DESERT COMMANDERS
The Men Who Served the Desert Fox,
North Africa, 1941–42
Samuel W. Mitcham Jr.
978-0-8117-3510-0

EXIT ROMMEL
The Tunisian Campaign, 1942–43
Bruce Allen Watson
978-0-8117-3381-6

THE WAR AGAINST ROMMEL'S SUPPLY LINES
1942–43
Alan J. Levine
978-0-8117-3458-5

THE EARLY BATTLES OF EIGHTH ARMY
Crusader to the Alamein Line, 1941–42
Adrian Stewart
978-0-8117-3536-0

WWW.STACKPOLEBOOKS.COM